Spinner's End by Rebecca Routh-S

Spinner's End

A Collection Of Poems

By Rebecca Routh-Sample

Spinner's End by Rebecca Routh-Sample

All rights reserved. This book or any portion thereof may not be produced in any manner without the express written permission of the author. Brief quotations are okay in review.

ISBN 978-1-4457-9574-4

Copyright 2024 by Rebecca Routh-Sample

Published 2024 by Lulu Press Inc

Spinner's End by Rebecca Routh-Sample

Other books by Rebecca Routh-Sample

Fiction

Diary Of A Teenage Fangirl

Diary Of A Teenage Rebel Girl   *Poetry*

ghost world

donnie darko

paramour

Spinner's End

The Greatest Love Story Never Told

Maybe You Never Loved Me As Much As You Loved New York

If You're Reading This, I Have Some Questions

All available to purchase on www.lulu.com and www.Amazon.com

Spinner's End by Rebecca Routh-Sample

Connect with me on social media if you want! I'd love to hear your feedback:

Twitter: @itsbeccafy

Instagram: @beccafyofficial

TikTok: @itsbeccafy

Spinner's End by Rebecca Routh-Sample

Contents

1, Spinner's End

2. True Love

3. To Be Loved Is To Be Changed

4. Cup Of Tea?

5. Wildflowers

6. Waving Through A Window

7. Tell Me Why

8. Brave

9. If You Were Mine

10. Where Did You Go?

11. Snowglobes

12. Replace You

13. Child

14. The Good One

15. Oh, What a World

16. Only You

Spinner's End by Rebecca Routh-Sample

17. Lifetime

18. Jealousy

19. I've Done Bad Things

20. Forever Friend

21. Things I Know To Be True

22. Who's Gonna Save You This Time?

23. The Long Game

24. The Last Page

Spinner's End by Rebecca Routh-Sample

Spinner's End

Lilly, I'll be waiting at Spinner's End I'll be

running up those hills

We'll never be running up again

Lilly, there's a daisy waiting for you

Lilly, if you only knew the depth of my

devotion drown in the Atlantic ocean

If I only knew

I'd brew a potion

Lilly, between the creeping branches and the

cliffside pools

My tears hold all my love for you

Before you ask if it's true

If you only knew

If you only knew

Spinner's End by Rebecca Routh-Sample

The Dark side enveloped me like a sickness Ate me from the inside out

Blacked out the pictures

And I bled out all over

my skin

Sectum Sempra

If only I didn't have such a bad temper

These are the days you can't get back

These are the words you can't take back

And I'll do my very best to keep what's

left of you alive

I feel it in my blood all the time

I'll tell every single lie over again

And I'll meet you on the other side

Not just in my head

We're not playing playground games

anymore

Spinner's End by Rebecca Routh-Sample

Washed away like sidewalk chalk   What

I wouldn't give

to relive it all

There comes a time in life

You don't realise

It's the last time you'll play outside

Until then

I'll see you on the other side

True Love

True love isn't violent

True love is kind

It's in your heart

Fizzing in the back of your mind

True love is pain like window pane   looking at the city at the

Spinner's End by Rebecca Routh-Sample

people all around you are they

gonna be okay?

True love isn't greedy

True love doesn't boast

True love isn't being a fixer and

raising a fake toast True love is

compassion for your fellow man try

to understand and communicate

the best you can   True love is an

advocate True love really cares

True love is stripping away

capitalist ideology and seeing

what's

really there Jesus forgave the sinners

and loved everyone he flipped

over the table in the temple and

gave as much as he could to

anyone

Spinner's End by Rebecca Routh-Sample

It was about giving all you had
help your fellow man the
golden rule we've forgotten
now these Conservative fake
prophets in a one horse town
and monetising hatred
promoting greed don't care
about what other people need
or hungry mouths to feed who
do we disdain today? Could be
doing so much good in the
world but you're just spreading
out pain
Jesus would be ashamed

To Be Loved Is To Be Changed

I'll always remember the 7/11
getting sprite and a can of
coke I was laughing because I

Spinner's End by Rebecca Routh-Sample

love you Not just because you
told a joke And that feeling
was in my heart and my red
cheeks Could barely see you
through the smoke

You kiss me You taste like
nicotine and teenage dreams I
never knew anything could
ever be like this My high school boyfriend never
appreciated my sacrifice My first love was simply a fool
A girl put her ambitions before my sanity

I'd do it all again

If it led me to you

Yes, I used to be thinner

My ego used to be bigger

But I didn't know what
true love would be Yes I
was perfect

Spinner's End by Rebecca Routh-Sample

Yes I was on time

But at night time

I would always feel sick

I'm calm enough to change my name

And I'd wait all day for that train

They say I'm going insane

But love is to be changed

God knows I love you

God knows I hate you

God knows you drive me insane

God knows my true feelings

God sees everything

I feel nothing but gratitude

I do it again

I'd die if led me to you

Spinner's End by Rebecca Routh-Sample

Cup Of Tea?

I keep waiting for someone to tell
me how they perceive me so I
can know that I exist and that
someone might need me I need
them to see me when I look in

the mirror
I don't know what I'm seeing wish
I knew what I was feeling I ask
everyone I know how I'm being
Do return the greeting?
Who am I? this bag of
flesh a hypochondriac
Aquarius moon mess a
vile creature from the
depths of hell vapid
bleach blonde corporate
shell

Spinner's End by Rebecca Routh-Sample

I think I'm a robot who can tell?

maybe you're a robot as well

robots can't bleed cut my

wrists open just to feel

something but i don't feel a

thing I see red as it pours out

of me but I don't feel angry

should I feel angry?

or apathy? cup of

tea? cup of tea?

Wildflowers

Wildflowers on my phone case wildflowers in my hair wildflowers by my beside I live without a care she walks by wildflowers in her hair walking up the spiral staircase there she goes again wildflowers when she

Spinner's End by Rebecca Routh-Sample

met me carnations when she left roses
when she loved me
lillies after death sunflowers on my
birthday and daisies when it's fair
snowdrops when it's rainy black
dahlia, you don't care willow tree
remembers the pear tree is right
there life gave you lemons and you
make lemonade   sitting under that
lemon tree in strawberry fields your
sweetness will the death of me

Waving Through A Window

I lost my mind over you   I'd
take a life for you

I'd wait all day in the rain to show
i'm in insane I'll never ever say

Spinner's End by Rebecca Routh-Sample

sorry because i won't take the
blame and when they curse your
name I'll take the pain novocaine
sinner's judgment days spent
and repent your crazy fucking
brain

my   dissent   is
treacherous   like gravity
          pulling me back
          down   again
pulling me back down
again pulling me back
down my fairweather
friend I haunt you like
a ghoul I never left I
drank your blood and
pushed you down and
went to count my

Spinner's End by Rebecca Routh-Sample

pennies up and spend

my days and nights

taking ownership of

my own torment peter,

won't you just let me

in? and the joy i bring

let   me   in   waving

through a window like a

widow

Tell Me Why

Where have you been?

I've been waiting for you such a long time

Come sit down, tell me why

I know you're out there

You're just hard to find

They tell me you're not real

Spinner's End by Rebecca Routh-Sample

I know they're lying

Where have you been all my life?

I know its took a long time

But you're here now, dry your eyes

I swear everything will be alright

Kathy lost on the moors

While Heathcliff waits at home

I've climbed mountains and rivers in my mind

But you were waiting in the castle in the sky

And every misadventure has led me closer to you

I feel every heartbreak break in two

Another lonely road

But I know where it goes

Wild man, kind man, hard man, soft man

You've made mistakes that have torn you in two   Rich man, poor man, wise man, tired man

You've made mistakes that have turned yourself blue

Spinner's End by Rebecca Routh-Sample

I will wait forever for you

If you wait for me too

You've been running from me all this time

Come in tell me why

I've been waiting for you all my life

But I'd do it every time

Brave

I've always been a coward

I could talk behind a keyboard for hours, and if I told truths out of my two pink lips   I'd be scared Id loose my power theres a right time for everything   but there is no right time for fate, it catches up quickly, and even comes to

Spinner's End by Rebecca Routh-Sample

those who wait and it can give you heaven, or disaster or on a plate, but either way, you know what you have to do?

You have to be brave

If You Were Mine

They don't know you like I do They think

we're both insane

I'd fight and kill and maim

Just to keep you safe

Trade my life for yours

Whatever it takes

Nobody's ever gonna hurt you But

I just have to grit my teeth

Because you're not with me

Spinner's End by Rebecca Routh-Sample

I hope she treats you kindly

But just remember

I would never hide my face when I'm around you

I'd hold you proudly 'cause you're mine

I'd share of my secrets

And I'd always have the time

I'd never let nobody hurt you

And if you were mean, I would be kind

Thats how I'd treat you

If you were mine

Where Did You Go?

What happened to you?

Where did you go?

Write your name in the snow

Spinner's End by Rebecca Routh-Sample

It used to be forever, you're here but you're not who I used to know

Where did you go?

Do I regret saving you? because I thought that meant saving you for myself now you're running around with her lesson learned that lights shine bright for everyone- not just for you It's not like I tried to put out your flame out as I was playing games you were playing games

and they were speculating but they don't really know your lovers name, do you even know who you're dating? Go out get drunk in the city do anything but be with me go to those parts of town and pray nobody sees you while I paint on a smile and on my phone I dial you, but there is no answer tell me the answer

Snowglobes

We were in a snow globe with our hands tied

there was truth in the white lies that we told over

and over again I watched you shining you saw

me crying we didn't know if our love would win

Spinner's End by Rebecca Routh-Sample

you took my hand and told me

it would be alright it would be

easy to run away from the

limelight and the highlights

and I said take me away from this cold

place the frost has numbed my face I

can't feel my lips

I can't feel the taste get me

out of here

I'm just spinning around the snow

globe will smash as I go down and so

it goes only our close friends know

the flashing lights and get black tights

leave me comatose but you know you

to heal me you know how to steal me

and take me to a place

Spinner's End by Rebecca Routh-Sample

nobody knows

keep me warm glue me back
together when i'm torn turn me
golden when i'm blue
I just wanna be with you

Replace You

You loved her

But you chose the money

And I don't find it funny

She never set rules when it came to love

But now she's shattered and the gates locked shut
You're a bad woman, you should've known better

She loved you even when you were her scarlet letter

You should've said no, shame on you now

Spinner's End by Rebecca Routh-Sample

Burning polaroids and golden tattoos now

Could've changed the world, now it's drenched in heartbreak

Dancing in the dark wasn't your only mistake

You should've called her

On the 28th night of September

When you were too drunk to remember

You were sworn to somebody else

You should've told her the truth

That there was no one who could ever ever ever

Replace you

But the damage has been done

And you'll lie and lie, next to another one

And your secrets splashed on the news front page

But you'll run away, on your getaway

Spinner's End by Rebecca Routh-Sample

Wasn't it better in your firefly catching days

Sparks flew every Fourth of July

Your the American Dream, turned to an Unbreakable Nightmare

She lies in bed on another continent

Trying to hold back tears through the blank stare

You'll still got time to change your mind

People do it all the time

You still have time to make it right

Or you'll regret it your whole

life

Child

So I stopped checking up on you

Because I've got better things to do

Spinner's End by Rebecca Routh-Sample

and if you want to be a child then I'll

leave the games to you because if you

don't really care then why the hell

should I?

I'd be there to wipe your tears, but who will wipe mine if not I?

I would've gave my life for you, whispers didn't matter...

If you don't reply, why the hell should I?

I'm not sending smoke signals,

I sending direct lines, and if you can't flick through yellow

paper to find a way of reply well you're dumb as well as

blind to let someone like me pass by

So I'm waving goodbye, I'm waving goodbye,

finding another place without fears and lies, a

place that needn't anyone, anyone but me, a

place that only a should see, a place just for me

I'm gonna find myself this time, but before

I can meet myself and say hello,

Spinner's End by Rebecca Routh-Sample

I need to say goodbye

You see you had me questioning who I was- who I am

myself, so I'm leaving you in bad times on bad lines

written in a book of lies, on a shelf, for unfortunate

souls

who believe popular opinion and believe the hype, I'll keep my secrets close and my truths closer, and escape into the night, and by the clapping of hooves

I'll leave those bastards behind

YOU'RE A CHILD

YOU'RE A CHILD

The Good One

Once upon a time there was a girl who lived in a small town in the North

And every time she dared to dream a bigger dream they scoffed

She would always be poor and worthless, she was taught

Spinner's End by Rebecca Routh-Sample

Under the thumb of the wicked witch, she thought

But what she didn't realise is she could save the kingdom and the people in it

Steal from the rich, take freedom and win it

People only stay small if you don't let them grow

So she'd thought she'd let them all know

Most people are bad people, thats just a fact

It can get disheartening, realising that

But there's one thing you've got that they don't have

You're a good one

And lay your head down on the pillow every night and know that

That's the power they don't have

Oh, What a World

People stay together out of convenience

Spinner's End by Rebecca Routh-Sample

Women agree with men because its easier

People are afraid to speak because of online hate I'm afraid to love so I sit and wait

Oh isn't it sad, but isn't it true?

The contradictions of this world turn is blue

Oh isn't it sad, but isn't it true?

These double standards are hard to say but true

If only we lived in a world

Where we could say

What we're afraid to and

Be heard

If only we lived in a world

Not built on cruelty

Or the shared experience

Of the privileged minority

But on universal truth

Oh, what a world

Spinner's End by Rebecca Routh-Sample

I stick by the things I say   I've

lost many friends that why   I

don't arse-kiss and I don't lie   I

don't care about your money

when you have no pride **Only**

You

Sometimes I wonder if I'm a bit too much Do other people fall so deeply in love?

Sometimes I wonder if I'm too emotional   Every time you leave, it kills me to see you go

Sometimes I wonder if love is too much for me

Can't sleep, can't breathe when you're not with me

But I fall hopelessly, recklessly hard as I can

Sometimes I wonder if I'm moving t oo fast?

Only you, only you can tell me that

Spinner's End by Rebecca Routh-Sample

Lifetime

Deep blue mountain smile

Stay with me just for a while

In the jet black night when the city's asleep

I'm wishing dreaming hoping you're thinking of me The cool wind brushes against the autumn leaves

The tides change with the moon like your feelings for me

Sacred heart, angel heart

Let it beat just for me

Safety lines, warning signs

Promise you'll only listen to me

Every night, the stars will shine

As I run through every singe lifetime

Every blissful night, you're my lifeline

And I pray I wake up next to you this time

Spinner's End by Rebecca Routh-Sample

The city murmurs, all in your head

Restlessness, in your bed

Tie your shoes, run down the street

The cobblestones where we used to meet

Fast ain't fast enough

Time ain't long enough

I just need you here with me

Lights flash, the stars will shine

Chasing cars between the fragile lines Been waiting all my life

For a perfect summer starcross'd night

And you've just been waiting for a meaning in life
Switching sides, the petty fights It all led up to this, right?

It made sense why she had to go

I keep a secret nobody knows

That I've always been in love with you

Spinner's End by Rebecca Routh-Sample

As sure as your eyes are hazel, and mine baby blue

From the first time I saw you

Hit me in the arrow in the back of my neck

Hurts so much that you're better off dead

But I will take the pain instead

Because I'll be healed on the day we wed

Dim the spotlight

Close the curtain

Final page, lessons learned 'n'

Divine intervention, what we're hoping

After the sun sets we'll be gold and

Grow old together

Rainy sunshine stormy weather

Sickness and health, we melt together

Come what may, come whatever

There's nothing longer than forever

Spinner's End by Rebecca Routh-Sample

This lifetime

Run through the fields of trees

Only to fall to your knees

Was it worth it? Wait and see

Don't make a mistake on me

Jealousy

I see you with him

My fingers trembling

This charade has gone to far

I'm bleeding out, screaming out   Windows down, no one hears a sound

In the backseat of my car

I can't believe it

Can't unsee it

Spinner's End by Rebecca Routh-Sample

What the hell do you think you're doing?

What about the love we made you just ruined

What about the life we built you said screw it

What about the ties to my heart? You undo it

What about the lies we tell

You can't do it anymore

Then tell me what were doing this for?

They'll never believe that it was all a ruse

The hardest thing to believe is the truth You're considering being his bride

But if we end up in smoke it'll all be fine

But you'll never be able to forget the 2AMs and the wildest summer nights

The sea, the sun, the waves and the tides

You held me all night and then I cried

Spinner's End by Rebecca Routh-Sample

I've Done Bad Things

I've done bad things so
have you I take my pills
and disappear from view
I'm honest but no one
believes me   I'm callous but
no one can feel me

I look sweet   but taste
like coal I look awake
but I'm comatose I cut
my skin but there's only
bone I'm a skeleton with
a heart of stone you try
to figure me out but I'm
unfathomable I tell you
sweet nothings but they
taste like salt dissolve

Spinner's End by Rebecca Routh-Sample

on your tounge and

fizzle out I take my pills

and howl at the moon I

scream into the dark I

scream at you

I scream at my life

I scream at time

I scream at my nightmares and open my eyes what an

earth are we doing, if we only die?

Forever Friend

Life is that thing you hold it

in the palm of your hand

but you let go and let it

pass you by trying to iron

out the wrinkles in time

separate colours fold it all

up phases like partners in

Spinner's End by Rebecca Routh-Sample

crime but all it is a jumbled

up mess

It's every friday you've ever spent wishing

for the weekend

It's the honeymoon that you wish

would never end

It's death that creeps up like sweet

revenge

It's the last few moments you'll ever

spend trying to recount the last

words said the longest three

seconds when you see your friend

and realize your love you dove into

the deep end more than a friend

the happy end the never end the

time you spend forever friend

you're my forever friend

Spinner's End by Rebecca Routh-Sample

Things I Know To Be True

There's so many things in life that change my moods,
the weather you know that I never stay in the same
place but no matter what

I know that wisdom comes with age I'm not afraid of
dying nothing more tiring than lying especially under a
man that doesn't know your worth that betrayals gonna

hurt these are the only things that I know
to be true

these are the only things
that I know to be true and
one of them is you

Who's Gonna Save You This Time?

If I could hold you this time I
missed you back then but I didn't

Spinner's End by Rebecca Routh-Sample

know why our hearts shattered in a pattern and dust turned into lies you need a white knight but who's gonna save you this time? you can hurt me all you like I ain't running come back running to me always on the

chase crash your car into me between the lies who's gonna save you this time? and the hopeless ever after you on the run but can't go faster paper houses in beverly hills famous before your time your jokes weren't funny and you took the money who's gonna save you this time? who's gonna save you? When the world is ending fading into ashes and dust and

Spinner's End by Rebecca Routh-Sample

your sweet, sweet talking ain't
doing enough and you're a car
crash honey

The Long Game

I'm playing the long game made my way round the
hard way who needs luck and daisy chains when
you've got the moral high ground and you're keeping
all the scores of the the games we play And the
ones who should be afraid aren't the ones that
crossed you but those that treat people like shit as if

that would see them through you
need talent, kindness and poise for
the stars to shine on you
So I'm playing the long game
I'm not gonna get him the wrong way
I'm doing things the right way
So I can sleep at night

Spinner's End by Rebecca Routh-Sample

The Last Page

Don't read the last page

But I marry you

And our dreams come true

I love you

I'm finally happy

All the money in the world

Can't replace the girl

Spinner's End by Rebecca Routh-Sample

Spinner's End by Rebecca Routh-Sample

All rights reserved. This book or any portion thereof may not be produced in any manner without the express written permission of the author. Brief quotations are okay in review.

ISBN 978-1-4457-9574-4

Copyright 2024 by Rebecca Routh-Sample

Published 2024 by Lulu Press Inc

Spinner's End by Rebecca Routh-Sample